DESTINATION
AUSTRALIA

The Twelve Apostles, southwest of Melbourne.

DESTINATION
AUSTRALIA

Photographs: Ernst Hermann Ruth
Text: Klaus Viedebantt
Birgit Gerke

WINDSOR BOOKS
INTERNATIONAL

Ayers Rock is one of Australia's most impressive and scenic splendours.

CONTENTS

A view from Centrepoint Tower out over the city centre and harbour of Sydney.

AUSTRALIA – "THE LUCKY COUNTRY"

The Secret Capital

"Sydbourne" is how Australians sometimes self-mockingly refer to their land. They are alluding to the fact that around forty percent of the some seventeen million "Aussies" reside in Sydney and Melbourne in the southeast corner of their vast and, for the most part, inhospitable continent. The two cities are respectively the capitals of New South Wales and Victoria. Indeed, the inhabitants of these two federal states alone amount to almost seventy percent of the fifth continent's population. It is no surprise then that the two cities are rivals. Neither city was prepared to allow the other to attain the status of federal capital when the Commonwealth of Australia was founded at the end of the last century. So, at a respectable distance from Sydney and Melbourne, the capital city of Canberra was created.

The rivalry between the two metropolises has continued as before until the present day, with Sydney more favourably positioned. It is not only its 3.5 million citizens who consider it the most beautiful city in the world, situated as it is around the splendid natural harbour that James Cook only just barely missed when he discovered the continent for England in 1770. The officers of the "First Fleet" were more fortunate when, in 1788, they established the first European settlement in "Sydney Cove", as a convict camp. This is where today's traffic accelerates across Circular Quay and where the ferries berth, after plying to and fro across the fifty-four square kilometres/twenty-one square miles of the bay. A pleasant way of getting to know Sydney is to take a trip around the harbour. The Quay is flanked by Australia's best known constructions: the Harbour Bridge, opened in 1932, and the Opera House, whose daring architecture has made it an international symbol, just as it has characterized Australia's new cultural awareness and self-confidence. Among the pioneers, these were qualities that for a long time were conspicuous by their absence.

The history of this architectural jewel is evidence of the bourgeois mentality of Sydney's citizenry that came close to thwarting the plans submitted by the Danish architect Jörn Utzon. He intended his building to appear as a ship setting out across the harbour with its sails billowing. For the man in the Sydney street, however, it was an "extravagant monstrosity". Annoyance escalated in line with rising building costs that in the end amounted to 102 million Australian dollars. Utzon himself faced so much hostility that he left Australia vowing never to return; and he did not relent even when Queen Elizabeth II, the Australian Head of State, opened the Opera House in 1973. Nowadays, it is difficult to find any Sydneysider (as the city's residents call themselves) who is not enormously proud of Utzon's masterpiece.

In contrast, next to no controversy accompanied the opening of the Harbour Bridge in 1932. Its main arch, 134 metres/440 feet in height, is nowadays dwarfed by the Sydney Tower which soars up 325 metres/1,066 feet, offering superb views out over the city harbour; over the bridge known affectionately as "the Coathanger"; over "The Rocks", the oldest part of Sydney that today is teeming with restaurants and stylish shops; over "Darling Harbour", the renovated and stylized dockland district now served by a sleek monorail; over the red-light district of King's Cross where heroin-trafficking has practically eliminated the area's former bohemian charm; over Taronga Zoo; over the famed, but often polluted, beaches of Bondi and Manly; and finally, toward the Blue Mountains in the distance. The tower is practically surrounded by the multi-storey headquarters of big business. In particular, it is the young and forward-looking economic enterprises that have established themselves in Sydney, much to the displeasure of Melbourne's city fathers.

The people of Melbourne regard this development as a threat to the traditional role of their city as the centre of the Australian economic and financial world. However, most of Melbourne's bankers and

A picnic in the centre of Sydney. A not atypical city worker's lunch break, since to drive across Sydney may take several hours.

economic leaders wave such apprehensions aside since they value the conservative, English atmosphere that prevails on the banks of the Yarra River. The metropolis of Melbourne, with its 3.1 million residents, can boast of ornamental façades dating back to the 1851 gold rush and subsequent commercial activity and decades of wealth. The city is endowed not only with Victorian elegance, not only with many parks and gardens, but also with artistic sensibility: the Victorian Arts Centre with its theatres and magnificent Art Museum is unequalled in Australia. Melbourne cherishes the European flair that may be seen not only in its nostalgic tramcars that have come to symbolize this town, but also in the elegant shopping passages of its city centre.

Kangaroos, Emus and Koalas

Melbourne, founded in 1835, is the ideal starting point for two trips that will acquaint visitor's with Australia's unique animal world, and yet neither involves a strenuous tour into the bush. The most worthwhile day tour is to Phillip Island, eighty kilometres/fifty miles from the city: here, visitors can see a colony of koalas living in the wild, a sight that has become all too rare. These delightful little creatures may be seen either snoozing or nibbling at their staple diet, the eucalyptus. Being marsupials, they have nothing in common with bears; nevertheless, they were the prototype of our beloved teddy bears. Equally delightful are the small fairy penguins which punctually at sunset waddle out of the sea into their burrows in the sand dunes. From nearby platforms, many tourists stand ready to enjoy this "penguin parade". The second tour, to Healesville Park, provides good opportunities for visitors to get a glimpse of Australia's most unusual animal, the "living fossil"of the duck-billed platypus. It resembles an otter with a beaver's tail and a duck's bill. It may be viewed paddling through an aquarium, while only a few metres away is its "biological brother", the spiny ant-eater. These are the only two of nature's egg-laying mammals and both may be seen in several Australian zoos. In Healesville, visitors can also walk about between uncaged kangaroos and emus, Australia's heraldic symbols. Snakes, of which Australia has a plentitude, are, however, kept behind glass, while nets strung high above hold in the continent's colourful bird world of parrots, cockatoos, laughing kookaburras and the beautiful lyrebird. One

may be fortunate enough to see this bird in the Dandenong Mountains, the nearby upland playground thronged at the weekend by sports enthusiasts from Melbourne.

Then, too, people crowd into the city's parks, especially into those lying along the Yarra River: on the left bank is the King's Domain with its Botanical Gardens, and on the right, Yarra Park which in 1956 was the site of the only Olympic Games ever held in Australia. Nowadays, in January, Yarra Park's state-of-the-art tennis stadium is where the world's tennis elite gathers for the Grand Slam tournament. Other parks are evocative of the nation's history: in Fitzroy Gardens there is a small building brought over from England, reputedly the house of James Cook's parents; in Carlton Gardens, there is the Royal Exhibition Building, where in 1901 the first Australian Parliament was convened.

A Capital in the Middle of Nowhere

It was not until 1927 that the Members of Parliament moved to a provisional building in Canberra that would, in fact, house them for the next six decades. In 1988, to mark Australia's Bicentenary, a gigantic flag was hoisted over the new Parliament House, thus realizing the designs for a federal capital submitted by the American architect Walter Burley Griffin in 1911; according to Griffin's model, Canberra was to be created from its humble base in the open countryside. Griffin divided the town from the government district by means of an artificial lake, but connected both parts by several streets which, like optical axes, converge on Parliament House on Capital Hill. Nature gradually softened the edges of Griffin's strict geometry, just as its close to 300,000 citizens gradually developed a feeling of identification with this new town. Although the number of tourists passing through annually outnumbers Canberra's residents, the city has retained its human dimension. Visitors are, above all, drawn to Parliament House, the Australian National Gallery and to the byzantine-styled bastion of the War Memorial, which is combined with a war museum. Particular emphasis is focused on historical representations of the 1915 Battle of Gallipolli, in which British commanders ordered their Australian und New Zealand soldiers to attack Turkish defensive positions, with a resultant high fatality rate. A national holiday still commemorates this tragic event, which gave rise in both Australia and Great Britain to an awareness of each country's national identity. Previously the Australians (as well as New Zealanders) had viewed themselves first and foremost as being "Britons in the South Seas".

Nowadays, members of the younger generation are proud to be "Aussies". For them, England is just a country like many others, apart from the fact that most people have a few relatives in the United Kingdom and that Queen Elizabeth II remains Australia's formal Head of State. The Australian flag still bears the Union Jack in addition to the Southern Cross. However, for years there has been continuing discussion as to whether or not Australia's new flag should bear the British emblem. Many citizens also favour new national colours, so that the present blue, white and red would be replaced by green and yellow, the colours already worn by Australians at international sporting events for a number of years. These colours are meant to recall the two typical Australian trees, namely the green leaves of the giant eucalyptus and the yellow blossoms of wattle trees, a type of acacia. Australians also debate whether their country should declare itself a republic. But the number of those who maintain loyalty to the Queen in London is still rather high, even among young Australians.

However, a quality which has been inherited from their predecessors is a scepticism toward "those in Canberra" and toward politics. It seems as if it is of no consequence whether the Labour Party or a coalition of Liberals and the Country Party is in power. Equally, the other great political power in the land, the trade unions with many card-carrying members, likewise do not enjoy unreserved approval since they often call for their members to lay down their tools purely on account of some trifle. The unions are only sure of support when, in times of economic recession, they attack the immigration quotas: Australia continues to be of prime attraction to immigrants from all over the world. However immigration has become increasingly difficult. Entry is allowed only to those who bring in enough money so as to create jobs, or to those specialists who can fill evident vacancies, for example in the electronics sector.

More recently, however, a different political issue has begun to be of more immediate concern to young voters, namely environmental protection. It was also in the smallest state that it first caused people to take to the streets. When plans were formulated to build a dam in the Tasmanian bush, the resulting protest campaign was such enough to cause every planner of large-scale projects throughout Australia to now take environmental considerations into account. It is indeed rare for so much awareness to be focused on Tasmania, but the controversy aroused by the projected dam of Gordon-below-Franklin was one of the few events which has caused the island off the southeast coast to become the centre of national attention. This has happened only twice before: in 1830, when a rugged convict colony was set up for particularly hardened criminals in Port Arthur; today the ruins are Tasmania's greatest tourist attraction. And in 1973, when Australia's first gambling casino was opened in the Tasmanian capital of Hobart. Meanwhile, roulette has been legalized in almost all states, while for a number of years, all the continent's gamblers had to make their way to Tasmania. The island benefited financially: as many players also brought their families along, Tasmania presented itself as a respectably bourgeois holiday destination. Nowadays, income obtained from tourism on the "Apple Island" is practically as important as its major economic sphere, fruit and vegetable cultivation.

German Wine for Australia's South

The industrialized state of South Austalia recognized the economic importance of tourism quite early, namely when Barossa Valley, not far from the capital Adelaide, realized that the many people visiting its vineyards provided good publicity for South Australian wine. It was the Australia's German immigrants who established these vineyards, and today everything German enjoys considerable popularity in this broad valley, be it "German schnitzel" or thigh-slapping Bavarian folk dancing. It was here that a development began which continues to contribute a substantial share to the volume of the national export trade; the good quality of Australian wine, which is now being produced not only in Barossa Valley, has come to be appreciated throughout the Pacific region. Even more significant, however, is the degree of acceptance that the wines have now achieved in the domestic market since Australians have long vied with Bavarians and Belgiums as the world's greatest beer drinkers. Though still a novelty in the country, small wine cellars have begun to appear in Adelaide, helping to make wine drinking socially acceptable. Frequently, it was artists and their coteries that preferred the beverage, much to the delight of the city fathers who consistently sought to use culture to improve Adelaide's mouse-grey reputation. In 1977, the city built its Festival Theatre, a modern complex standing on the banks of the Torrens River, consisting of two rather unusual white buildings; the Theatre plays host biennially to an internationally-recognized

View towards Centrepoint Tower from Bennelong Point, with the famous sail-roof of the Sydney Opera House.

Bowls is particularly popular with the older generation. There are bowling greens in many public parks throughout Australia.

Festival of Arts. The city, which as a centre of the automobile and electrical industries had achieved affluence, could well afford such an investment. The elegant capital, with its one million residents, did in fact profit considerably from the attention it attracted. But it was not only the new theatre which helped Adelaide: At a considerable financial outlay, the city bought the rights to hold the only Grand Prix motor racing championships held in Australia. Now a motor-racing circuit takes over the South Australian capital's broad streets, annually drawing publicity from around the world. The most recent project is a technology centre that is to be built by Japanese investors on the edge of town.

Australia's most famous road begins in Adelaide. The Stuart Highway traverses the entire continent: through South Australian deserts; past Coober Pedy, where men and women obsessively dig for opals and seek shelter from the scorching sun in subterranean quarters; via Alice Springs at the dry, torrid centre of the country; through the tropically humid mangrove swamps of the Northern Territory; and reaching the north coast at Darwin, the capital of the Northern Territory. Since 1988, the highway has had an asphalt surface for its entire length. As far as Alice Springs there is also a railway line that is used not only by freight trains but also by a legendary passenger train, "The Ghan". The road itself is named after John McDouall Stuart who, in 1861-1862, was the first explorer to traverse the continent from Adelaide to Darwin. It was thanks to his achievement that it was then possible to lay a telegraph line which was extended from Darwin to Indonesia and on to Britain, the "Mother Country". With this connection, Australia was linked to the rest of the world.

The Rock at the "Red Heart" of the Continent

Alice Springs came into being as a telegraph station. To Australians, this small town stands as a symbol of the outback, as the wilderness in Australia's interior is called, just as it symbolizes the pioneer courage, the "real Aussie spirit" that conquered that vast emptiness. The central location of Alice (as the town has been known ever since Neville Shute's bestseller *A Town Like Alice*) has made it the logical base for two national institutions, namely the "Royal Flying Doctor Service" and the "School of the Air". The flying doctors provide the remote sheep stations with medical services, while the school educates the children on the farms via two-way radios. Both institutions are included in the tourist programmes for the outback, tours that begin in Alice Springs. They continue on to

King's Canyon, take in a camel safari and, as their highlight, include a memorable visit to Ayers Rock, 448 kilometres/278 miles to the southwest, the most famous site on the continent.

The Aborigines living in the shadow of this gigantic rock know it as "Uluru". It rears up directly out of the flat plain and, according to the direction of the sun, changes its colour like a chameleon, from grey and violet to orange and bright red. As this 340 metre/1,115 foot high rock has been sacred to the Aborigines since the beginning of time, access to some of the caves and springs at the rock's base continues to be permitted only to tribal members. Ayers Rock is part of a national park, and a small hotel centre at the Yulara Tourist Village (with its own airport) has been built twenty kilometres/twelve miles away, outside the national park. The rock is encircled by a track nine kilometres/five-and-a-half miles long. An ascent up the rock's smooth flanks requires rather great exertion and can be tricky. However, the view from the top over the plains is indeed rewarding. The lofty domed tops of The Olgas can be seen some thirty-five kilometres/twenty-two miles away, a rock formation that many visitors consider even more attractive than the monolith named after Governer Ayers. Both are in Uluru National Park.

Although many tourists fly out to the rock, a good number make their way from Alice Springs aboard four-wheel-drive vehicles, allowing them something of an outback adventure. One of the routes to Alice passes by the missionary station of Hermannsburg, founded by German Lutherans who attempted to bring Christianity and agricultural skills to the Aborigines; special permission is required to visit the Hermannsburg settlement. Nearby is a memorial commemorating the settlement's most famous pupil, the painter Albert Namatjira, whose paintings may be seen in all important Australian museums. His story was typical among the Aborigines. Not until 1957, that is at the age of fifty-five and two years before his death, was he accorded the same rights enjoyed by every white Australian. His death was probably caused by alcoholism, an addiction the missionaries were as helpless against as are the present day authorities. It is still possible to meet up with the Aborigines of the outback and to become aware of the skills and qualities they have acquired amidst the seemingly hostile bush country. Once one has gained some inkling of their poetic myths and even enjoyed their trusting friendliness, it is all the more difficult to associate them with the miserable forms of their fellow-Aborigines who are to be seen lying around in Australia's urban parks.

View across the Brisbane River of Brisbane's skyline, with its fascinating mixture of old and new architecture.

FLINDERS STREET STATION

| BELGRAVE · LILYDALE HEALESVILLE LINES | ALAMEIN LINE | FRANKSTON LINE MORNINGTON STONY POINT LINES | WILLIAMSTOWN ALTONA LINES | DANDENONG LINE (GENERAL MOTORS) | SANDRINGHAM LINE | BROADMEADOWS LINE | PORT MELBOURNE LINE | ST KILDA LINE |

*Main entra[nce]
of Melbourn[e's]
largest railw[ay]
station, Flin[ders]
Street Statio[n.]
Melbourne i[s a]
cosmopolita[n]
city with wi[de,]
tree-lined
boulevards.*

"Crocodile Dundee" Assists Tourism

It has repeatedly been the fate of Darwin, situated on the tropically humid north coast, to lie in the path chosen by destructive cyclones. "Tracy", as meteorologists had christened it, almost completely destroyed the town on Christmas Day 1974, as though in a replay of the Japanese 1942-1943 bombing raids which took a toll of two thousand lives. Although not the first in the history of the town, the devastating storm made people in the Northern Territory reconsider whether it was worth attempting once again to rebuild their capital. They overcame their misgivings and this time opted for reinforced constructions that have so far withstood all climate rigours, though being no great delight for the eye. However, proliferating tropical plants and luxuriant tree growth have again endowed the town with character. This is of definite advantage in view of the growing tourist industry, brought on by "Crocodile Dundee", the Australian movie shot mainly in the Northern Territory; the film became a box-office hit worldwide. Consequently, tourists by the thousand wish to see crocodiles, and there is no short supply of them. Two species have their habitat along the north coast,

namely the Johnson crocodile, which grows up to three metres/ten feet long but constituting no danger to human beings, and the saltwater crocodile, growing up to seven metres/twenty-three feet in length. As these "salties" are quite partial to a diet that includes humans, they were well on their way toward being hunted to extinction when they were declared a protected species at the beginning of the 1970s. Now they can be encountered throughout the region, and especially in the beautiful Kakadu National Park, a much frequented attraction owing to its Aboriginal rock drawings.

The "crocs", of course, also wallow and romp in the rivers and ponds of northern Queensland, a region that currently is being increasingly opened up to tourism. Even at the not easily accessible northern end of the Cape York Peninsula, Australia's northernmost point, the first tourist hotel was built a few years ago. This fits in well with Queensland's image since for many Australians, this state is synonymous with holiday-making. The continent's most frequented bathing resorts are situated north and south of Brisbane, the territory's capital, on the Sunshine Coast and on the Gold Coast. The best-known area is Surfers Paradise, where the multi-storey hotels bring

to mind Spanish holiday resorts; as its name indicates, here is a resort offering more than just the chance to bathe. Surfing in warm, metre-high waves is one of the principal delights enjoyed by young "Aussies", while families are attracted to the broad beaches of fine sand where "life saving guards" conscientiously keep vigil. These young, athletic lifeguards, with their old-fashioned bathing caps fastened under their chins, are elite troops in the service of a beach-loving, leisure-oriented nation. To have won a prize at one of the very well attended life-saving competitions is seen as a life-time achievement. The lifeguards are there not only to help swimmers who have gotten into difficulties but also to be on the lookout for the stealthy approach of sharks.

Scientists are, however, of the opinion that the greatest peril to which one is exposed on Australia's beaches does not lurk in the water but is rather sunbathing itself: ozone depletion over the Antarctic has resulted in an increased exposure of the Fifth Continent to damaging ultraviolet rays, in turn, leading to the highest frequency of skin cancer being suffered by Australians. For this reason, numerous experts involved in skin cancer research number among the continent's medical authorities.

Scientific recognition is also accorded researchers in Brisbane. The city had formerly been a centre of gerontology studies, as Queensland's capital has enjoyed particular popularity from those who have retired. However, this city of one million residents stretching inland along the Brisbane River, has turned into one of the continent's fastest growing economic centres during the 1980s. This became particularly evident at the 1988 World Exhibition, which Brisbane held under the motto "Leisure in the Age of Technology", in part as a celebration of Australia's Bicentenary. High-tech industries have now become one of Queensland's prime sources of income in addition to agriculture (stock raising, suger-cane and tropical fruit), the mining of mineral deposits, and tourism. Many specialists also feel drawn to the city on account of its subtropical climate.

Coral – One of the Wonders of the World

The real South Sea idyll, truly tropical scenery, begins only north of the Tropic of Capricorn. The town of Rockhampton, lying directly on that latitude, marks the southernmost point of the Great Barrier Reef which is to be regarded among the wonders of the modern world. This, the world's largest coral reef, two thousand kilometres/twelve hundred miles long, is some 15,000 years old. Withstanding the assaults of our planet's most powerful ocean, it continues to shelter countless brilliantly coloured schools of fish and is a realm of plants and corals in a myriad of radiant hues.

Almost six hundred islands rise up out of flat turquoise shimmering lagoons, forming this wall which has been created by minute forms of life. There are coral islands that scarcely protrude above sea level, in addition to larger rocky islands such as the Whitsunday Group, the crests of a sunken hilly landscape. Some of the islands serve as holiday resorts with more or less sophisticated hotel facilities, small airstrips or helicopter landing pads, and with golf courses and swimming pools positioned alongside exquisitely beautiful palm-fringed beaches. South Sea dreams indeed, but which come at a price.

Just as the islands differ in appearance, so they appeal to different sorts of holiday-makers. While some, such as Lizard Island, are bare and with scenery of little interest, they do nevertheless provide anglers with access to unusual fishing grounds. Consequently, deep-sea anglers use Lizard Island as a base in their search for marlin. Other islands are overgrown with a thick, steaming jungle, covering all paths with lianas. Green Island and Heron Island are two pure coral islands that are protected nature reserves. Effective publicity has made some islands well known throughout Australia and correspondingly full of hustle and bustle, while others offer room to only two or three dozen guests. One quality that all have in common is that they make excellent bases for underwater adventures, be it equipped with a snorkel or with an oxygen supply. The Great Barrier Reef is indeed, at times, far distant, for in some places it is almost four hundred kilometres/two-hundred-fifty miles off the mainland, but there are fascinating coral gardens growing and proliferating around most of the islands.

In such sun-drenched waters fish and other marine life find ample nutrition. Nature is still intact here, even if it is not wholly unendangered. The two prime enemies are the crown-of-thorns starfish and man. The starfish suck the coral polyps out of their refuges, killing off the coral slowly but surely. There is no effective way of combating the starfish's depredations. Man, however, endangers this natural wonder in two different ways: hordes of tourists pollute the sea and often wantonly destroy the coral structures that have grown only very slowly over hundreds of years. The reef will face an even greater danger if, as

demanded in Queensland, drilling operation start to tap the oil reserves lying below the seabed. The authorities administering the national park to which a large part of the reef belongs would be not be able to protect the coral against the probable and unfortunate ravages of oil pollution.

From the Gold Rush to Uranium Row

On the other side of the continent, Western Australia's coast causes less concern to those ecologically minded, even though out in the Indian Ocean, Australia's largest natural gas field is being exploited. There are only a few coral reefs lying off the northwest corner of this coast. The Dutch explored this region at the beginning of the seventeenth century. They had come from their not far distant colonies in the East Indies, today's Indonesia. However, since the bare and torrid land promised these merchants neither lucrative exotic spices nor gold or other precious metals, they simply continued on their way. They had, though, set foot on the continent and named it "New Holland" at least a century-and-a-half before James Cook stepped ashore. Had Captain Dirk Hartog known that this apparently desolate land concealed immense mineral wealth, he surely would not have been content in 1616 merely to nail an engraved pewter plate to a post set up beside Western Australia's Shark Bay. Another three centuries were to pass before what are probably the world's largest iron ore deposits were discovered in northwestern Australia. The mining industry which this ore and other mineral wealth has brought into being has increased the population of Perth, the capital of Western Australia, to one million residents.

The fact that the city on the Swan River has grown rapidly is apparent: skyscrapers belonging to mining and insurance companies as well as banks contribute to its character. Nevertheless, daily life in Perth is not characterized by hectic hustle and bustle but rather by the relaxed atmosphere of a holiday resort.

This city, founded in 1829, is said to have the best climate of all the Australian state capitals and, in view of Australia's generally excellent weather, that is quite an admission. An average of eight hours sunlight are to be enjoyed here daily and even in July, the coldest winter month, the temperature is usually above 13° Celsius/55° Fahrenheit. Most important of all, however, is the cool breeze that wafts in on warm summer afternoons from the Indian Ocean some twenty kilometres/twelve miles away. The people of Perth have named the wind the "Fremantle Doctor" after the port at the mouth of the Swan.

Fremantle is entered into the world's sporting annals: in 1983, business tycoon Alan Bond from Perth succeeded in sailing his yacht "Australia II" to victory in the America's Cup off the coast of New England. For the first time in the 132 years of the Cup's history, it has been possible to steal the trophy from the United States. But four years later, off the coast of Fremantle, the loss was revenged, and the Australians surrendered the prize to the victorious American crew.

In spite of everything, Perth enjoyed hitting the headlines, since their town is the most isolated metropolis anywhere in the world, surrounded on one side by the Indian Ocean and on the other by a sheer never-ending desert. Western Australia, which alone is over ten times larger than Great Britain, has a population of merely 1.3 million, of which at least one million live in Perth.

If it had not been for the boom resulting from the exploitation of mineral wealth, the only big city on the west of the continent would hardly have grown so quickly. As with the states on the east coast, such growth here was also due to a gold rush. Back in the 1890s, gold was discovered far out into the west Australian desert, and thousands of fortune seekers,

undeterred by the absence of water and the scorching heat, moved onto the desert. The towns of Kalgoorlie and Collgardie came into being and started to provide increasing amounts of gold. Water supply pipes were laid from Perth to the two gold-fields some 550 kilometres/340 miles away. Today, Kalgoorlie is still supplied in this way and its gold mines continue to produce almost half of Australia's total gold.

However, gold has long ceased to have the importance that it once had for Australia. In the meantime, a great variety of ores, minerals and fossil fuels have been discovered on this island-continent. Australia appears, in effect, to consist exclusively of mineral wealth: in the east enormous coal seams are mined; in the northeast there is iron ore; and in many parts of the country, there is uranium. However, particularly at these mines there have already been numerous clashes. On the one hand there are groups opposing nuclear power and who therefore, do not wish uranium to be exported (Australia itself has no nuclear power stations), while on the other hand, there are the Aborigines. Many of the uranium mines are situated on land that belongs to the continent's original inhabitants. As the owners, the Aborigines

Sailing off Port Douglas, about seventy metres/forty-three miles north of Cairns. Boats circumnavigating the globe often make for Port Douglas.

often refuse to allow mining since the mines are in sacred areas.

As, however, the state has the right to exploit mineral wealth even on private ground, two mutually excluding stances stand opposed. Usually attempts are made to resolve such disputes by political means. Though from time to time there are disputes about other mineral deposits, it is usually those concerning uranium which make the headlines. Nevertheless, Australia is able to provide ores and mineral of the very best quality. For example in the north of Western Australia, one of the world's largest diamond fields is being exploited; Australia is also the world's leading supplier of bauxite, an ore mined in north Queensland.

Australia can live well from its mineral wealth since Asia's industrialized nations, technologically advanced but lacking raw materials, provide an assured market. Nevertheless, from time to time Australians are frightened out of their cosy existence as the prices for raw materials plummet on the world markets, causing Australia's balance of trade to fall into the red. Then, the weaknesses of the Australian economy again become visible since it depends too greatly on exporting raw materials and too little on the domestic production of competitive goods for world markets.

Australia had long protected its domestic market against cheaper Asiatic competition by means of high import tariffs. This was wholeheartedly supported by the influential trade unions, which were able to enjoy an equally pleasant existence shielded by high protective trade barriers, and which were extraordinarily ready to call strikes just to maintain the status quo. It was not until the 1980s, when the Asian countries increasingly urged Australia to admit their products, did Australia become obliged to change its policy, if only as a means of placating these most important export customers.

Lambs and Wool for Arabia and Asia

This development in Australia's trade policy was also strongly influenced by developments in the economy's second largest sector, namely agriculture. It was agriculture, and above all sheep breeding, that laid the foundations for the country's prosperity at the beginning of the nineteenth century, when the first shipments of wool were exported to Great Britain. A number of years had to pass, however, before the first refrigerator ships were transporting lamb, beef, butter and cheese to Britain.

From then on, the colony and later the Commonwealth of Australia, together with its neighbour New Zealand, provided the industrialized regions of the United Kingdom with meat and milk products. Such trade was as profitable as it was without problems, since at times there were close to one-hundred-fifty million sheep grazing on Australia's pasture lands.

All this changed when Britain joined the European Community and began to annually reduce its import quotas for agricultural products produced by countries outside the European Community. Australia was obliged to change its economic course. New customers had to be found in the previously neglected countries of Asia; the Arabs had to be persuaded to buy more sheep; and the multitudes of steak-eating Americans had to be convinced of the quality of Australian beef. Once again the high quality of Australian wool proved its importance to the Australian economy. The Soviet Union, the United States and Japan have become the country's largest wool customers, even if world prices for wool have also repeatedly hit rock bottom. Even in bad times when wool prices are low, almost one-hundred-thirty million sheep continue to munch on Australian grass, most of them on special farms with more than one-hundred-thousand animals. Some of these farms also accommodate tourists, or arrange demonstrations of their sheep dogs' skills. Sheep-breeding in Australia would be inconceivable without these dogs and without the cross-country motorcycles which the drovers race around the rough pasture grounds. Equally indispensable are the sheep shearers travelling across the land during the shearing season and setting up base on the sheep farms for a few days. It takes only a few minutes using electric shears for these professionals to divest a sheep of its fleece; the shearers are usually paid per sheep shorn. As in New South Wales and Victoria, sheep-farming is an important aspect of Western Australian agriculture.

From the Indian to the Pacific Ocean

The actually meaning of this title becomes apparent as one travels eastward on the "Indian Pacific": having crossed the mountain chain inland of Perth, one rolls through Western Australia's agricultural regions, first traversing Australia's granary, then through cattle and sheep pastures and finally into the savannah and deserts covering the greater part of the continent.

The transcontinental train, bearing the names of the oceans that it connects, needs two-and-a-half days to travel from Perth to Sydney. The railway has made an enormous contribution in connecting the west with the altogether more populated east. The two railway networks already in existence in the west and the east were first joined together in 1917. Some historians believe that if this connection had not been made, then Western Australia, which comprises one-third of the overall area of Australia, perhaps might have developed into a separate country.

Nowadays, the railway which crosses three time zones is mostly an attraction for tourists and railway enthusiasts: its most remarkable feature is that its tracks, lying between the scrawny bushes of the desolate Nullarbor Plain, extend 478 kilometres/297 miles in a seemingly unending, but utterly straight line, a world record.

Shortly before Sydney, the train, which is almost always booked out far in advance, reaches the Blue Mountains, part of that mountain range running parallel to the entire east coast. The mountains are the only sizeable elevation on what is the smallest of the world's continents. The 2,228 metre/7,310 foot high Mount Kosciusko, the highest mountain in Australia, is part of this mountain chain which extends down into Tasmania and, as scientists believe, connected once with the Antarctic mountains before the continents split apart millions of years ago. Nowaday, this massif, with its Snowy Mountains, offers the best ski areas in Australia.

In a earlier age, the mountains constituted a practically insurmountable obstacle to the country's first white settlers, the British convicts and their guards. As the narrow strip of land on the east coast did not provide enough to eat, it was urgently necessary to find a way through the mountains. In 1813, a group of four prisoners finally succeeded in locating a pass which led into the fertile land lying beyond the mountains. Convicts, promised their freedom upon completion of the work, built a road through the rough wilderness in record time. Hunger, the worst scourge confronting the convict colony, could now be overcome.

Gradually, it also became possible to establish a more civilized way of life. And now, for the first time, free settlers came, of their own volition, to the country that hitherto had only been of bad repute. Australia began to prosper and became one of the countries most favoured worldwide by emigrants, a popularity that has continued unbroken despite the continent's economic problems. For hundreds of thousands of people hailing from the four corners of the globe, the Fifth Continent continues to remain what it has always been for its people, namely "The Lucky Country".

The Ormiston Gorge in the MacDonnell Ranges, west of Alice Springs, unites gullies and watercourses in the red heart of Australia in a unique and scenic beauty.

Green Island, a genuine coral island and part of the Great Barrier Reef, is a nature reserve.

Near Cooma, south of Canberra. In view of the drought conditions, it is difficult to believe that grazing is possible here.

DOWN UNDER – THE FIFTH CONTINENT

Australia in Narratives and Reports

That Australia continues to present a rough and rugged environment is a fact that cannot be disputed. Its outback remains an unsettled and hostile environment and will likely remain this way. The extent of nature's ravages are brought to light by our excerpts below, taken from the writings and dairies of Australia's early explorers. Some ideas from the continent's first settlers are also included along with some more light-hearted reflections by Australian-born writers. To complete our anthology, a few more modern writings, one concerning the Aboriginal population, are included. While the texts may further instill the idea of a wild and untamed paradise, perhaps they are just what is required to pull some of us toward the expanse.

Tasmania, 1642

They [the sailors sent ashore] had heard certain human sounds, and also sounds nearly resembling the music of a trump, or a small gong, not far from them, though they had seen no one. ...

They had seen two trees about 2 or 2 1/2 fathom in thickness, measuring from 60 to 65 feet from the ground to the lower-most branches, which trees bore notches made with flint implements, the bark having been removed for the purpose. These notches, forming a kind of steps to enable persons to get up the trees and rob the birds' nests in their tops, were fully 5 feet apart, so that our men concluded that the natives here must be of very tall stature, or must be in possession of some sort of artifice for getting up the said trees. In one of the trees these notched steps were so fresh and new that the seemed to have been cut less than four days ago. ...

On the ground they had observed certain footprints of animals, not unlike those of a tiger's claws.

In 1642, the Dutch navigator ABEL JANSZOON TASMAN (1603?-1659) discovered Tasmania and New Zealand, having circumnagivated Australia. Tasman was in the service of the Dutch East India Company.

The Unfrightened Natives

There were 10 or 12 of the Natives a little way off, who seeing us three going away from the rest of our Men, followed us at a distance. I thought they would follow us: But there being for a while a Sand-bank between us and them, that they could not then see us, we made a halt, and hid our selves in a bending of the Sand-bank. They knew we must be thereabouts, and being 3 or 4 times our Number, thought to seize us. So they dispers'd themselves, some going to the Sea-shore, and others beating about the Sandhills. We knew by what Rencounter we had had with them in the Morning that we could easily out-run them. So a nimble young Man that was with me, seeing some of them near, ran towards them; and they for some time, ran away before him. But he soon over-taking them, they faced about and fought him. He had a Cutlass, and they had wooden Lances; with which, being many of them, they were too hard for him. When he first ran towards them I chas'd two more that were by the Shore: But fearing how it might be with my young Man, I turn'd back quickly, and went up to the top of a Sandhill, whence I saw him near me, closely engag'd with them. Upon their seeing me, one of them threw a Lance at me, that narrowly miss'd me. I discharg'd my Gun to scare them, but avoided shooting any of them; till finding the young Man in great danger from them, and my self in some; and that tho' the Gun had a little frighted them at first, yet they had soon learnt to despise it, tossing up their Hands, and crying Pooh, Pooh, Pooh; and coming on afresh with a great Noise, I thought it high time to charge again, and shoot one of them, which I did. The rest, seeing him fall, made a stand again; and my young Man took the Opportunity to disengage himself, and come off to me.

WILLIAM DAMPIER (1652-1715) was appointed to the English Admiralty to command an expedition to the South Seas. He became the first Englishman to explore the west coast of Australia.

Communities along the Stuart Highway often consist of nothing more than a filling station and a few houses, as here in Kulgera, nearly three hundred kilometres/one hundred-ninety miles south of Alice Springs.

On the Great Northern Highway between Halls Creek and Fitzroy Crossing. The three hundred kilometre/one hundred-ninety mile dirt track crosses rivers and is at times closed due to flooding.

The Murray River

It was with considerable apprehension that I observed the river to be shoaling fast, more expecially as a huge sand-bank, a little below us, and on the same side on which the natives had gathered, projected nearly a third-way across the channel. To this sand-bank they ran with tumultuous uproar, and covered it over in a dense mass. Some of the chiefs advanced to the water to be nearer their victims, and turned from time to time to direct their followers. With every pacific disposition, and an extreme reluctance to take away life, I foresaw that it would be impossible any longer to avoid an engagement, yet with such fearful numbers against us, I was doubtful of the result. The spectacle we had witnessed had been one of the most appalling kind, and sufficient to shake the firmness of most men; but at that trying moment my little band preserved their temper coolness, and if anything could be gleaned from their countenances, it was that they had determined on an obstinate resistance. But at the very moment, when my hand was on the trigger, and my eye was along the barrel, my purpose was checked by M'Leay, who called to me that another party of blacks had made their appearance upon the left bank of the river. Turning round, I observed four men at the top of their speed. The foremost of them as soon as he got ahead of the boat, threw himself from a considerable height into the water. He struggled across the channel to the sand-bank, and in an incredibly short space of time stood in front of the savage, against whom my aim had been directed. Seizing him by the throat, he pushed him backwards, and forcing all who were in the water upon the bank, he trod its margin with a vehemence and an agitation that were exceedingly striking. At one moment pointing to the boat, at another shaking his clenched hand in the faces of the most forward, and stamping with passion on the sand. ... The reader will imagine our feelings on this occasion: it is impossible to describe them. We were so wholly lost in interest at the scene that was passing, that the boat was allowed to drift at pleasure. For my own part I was overwhelmed with astonisment, and in truth stunned and confused; so singular, so unexpected, and so strikingly providential, had been our escape.

CHARLES STUART (1795-1869) was the discoverer of Australia's Darling River in 1828. In 1829-1830, he surveyed the Murrumbidgee and Murray Rivers,

Bush fire on Australia's southwest coast. The country's vegetation has adapted to the rhythmic pattern of fire and drought. The seed capsules of many plants do not germinate until a bush fire has caused them to open.

an expedition which, given the harsh conditions, he and his companions were lucky to survive.

The Great Sandy Desert

A strong east wind is blowing. We are compelled to give up smoking whilst on short allowance of water. It is a deprivation, for smoke and water stand in the place of food. We started west-south-west at 6.30 p.m., and made twenty-five miles, though we had most trying sand-hills to cross. I became quite unable to continue the journey, being reduced to a skeleton by thirst, famine, and fatigue. I was so emaciated and weak I could scarcely rise from the ground, or stagger half a dozen steps when up. Charley had been absent all day, and we were alarmed about him when he did not return at sunset. I knew not what to do. Delay was death to us all, as we had not water enough to carry us through; on the other hand, to leave the camp without the lad seemed an inhuman act, as he must then perish. It was six against one, so I waited till the moon was well up, and started at 9 p.m. We made about eight miles, and whilst crossing a flat heard, to our intense delight, a 'cooee', and Charley joined us. Poor lad, how rejoiced we were to

see him again so unexpectedly! The lad had actually walked about twenty miles after all the fatigue of the previous night's travelling; he had run up a large party of natives, and gone to their water. This news of more water permitted us to use at once what we had with us, and the recovery of Charley put us in good spirits. It may, I think, be admitted that the hand of Providence was distinctly visible in this instance. I had deferred starting until 9 p.m., to give the absent boy a chance of regaining the camp. It turned out afterwards that had we expedited our departure by ten minutes, or postponed it for the same length of time, Charley would have missed us; and had this happened there is little doubt that not only myself, but probably other members of the expedition would have perished from thirst. The route pursued by us was at right angles with the course taken by the boy, and the chances of our stumbling up against each other in the dark were infinitesimally small. Providence mercifully directed it otherwise, and our departure was so timed that, after travelling from two to two hours and a half, when all hope of the recovery of the wanderer was almost abandoned, I was gladdened by the 'cooee' of the brave lad, whose keen ears had caught the sound of the bells attached to the camels' necks. To the energy and courage of this untutored native may, under the guidance of the Almighty, be attributed the salvation of the party. It was by no accident that he encountered the friendly well. For fourteen miles he followed up the tracks of some blacks, though fatigued by a day of severe work, and, receiving a kindly welcome from the natives, he had hurried back, unmindful of his own exhausted condition, to apprise his companions of the important discovery he had made. We turned towards the native camp, and halted a short distance from it, that we might not frighten them away. I was so utterly exhausted when we camped, at 3 a.m., that it was evident I never could have gone on after that night without more food and water. I would therefore thankfully acknowledge the goodness and mercy of God in saving my life by guiding us to a place where we got both.

In April 1873, the Australian explorer PETER EGERTON WARBURTON (1813-1889) set off from Alice Springs with an aim of reaching the Indian Ocean. When the company reached Oakover River on 21 January 1874, they became the first men to cross the continent from east to west. This journal entry was made on 5 November 1873.

Reaching the Sea, 1862

Thursday, 24th July, Thring Creek. Entering the Marsh. Started at 7.40, course north. I have taken this course in order to make the sea coast, which I suppose to be distant about eight miles and a half, as soon as possible; by this I hope to avoid the marsh. I shall travel along the beach to the north of the Adelaide. I did not inform any of the party, except Thring and Auld, that I was so near to the sea, as I wished to give them a surprise on reaching it. ... At eight miles and a half came upon a broad valley of black alluvial soil, covered with long grass; from this I can hear the wash of the sea. On the other side of the valley, which is rather more than a quarter of a mile wide, is growing a line of thick heavy bushes, very dense, showing that to be the boundary of the beach. Crossed the valley, and entered the scrub, which was a complete network of vines. Stopped the horses to clear a way, whilst I advanced a few yards on to the beach, and was gratified and delighted to behold the water of the Indian Ocean in Van Diemen Gulf, before the party with the horses knew anything of its proximity. Thring, who rode in advance of me, called out, 'The Sea!' which so took them all by surprise, and they were so astonished, that he had to repeat the call before they fully understood what was

meant. Then they immediately gave three long and hearty cheers. ... After all the party had had some time on the beach, at which they were much pleased and gratified, they collected a few shells; I returned to the valley, where I had my initials (J.M.D.S.) cut on a large tree, as I did not intend to put up my flag until I arrived at the mouth of the Adelaide. Proceeded on a course of 302° along the valley; at one mile and a half, coming upon a small creek with running water, and the valley being covered with beautiful green grass, I have camped to give the horses the benefit of it. Thus have I, through the instrumentality of Divine Providence, been led to accomplish the great object of the expedition, and take the whole party safely as witnesses to the fact, and through one of the finest countries man could wish to behold – good to the coast, and with a stream of running water within half a mile of the sea. From Newcastle Water to the sea-beach, the main body of the horses have been only one night without water, and then got it within the next day. If this country is settled, it will be one of the finest Colonies under the Crown, suitable for the growth of any and everything.

JOHN McDOUALL STUART (1815-1866) was the first man to reach the centre of Australia, in 1860, and in 1862, the first to cross the continent from south to north. He reached the goal only at a great cost to his health: he lost the power of speech and went blind, before dying four years later.

The Gibson Desert, 1874

About the 29th I had emptied my keg, and was still over twenty miles from the Circus. Ah! who can imagine what twenty miles means in such a case? But in this April's ivory moonlight I plodded on, desolate indeed, but all undaunted, on this lone, unhallowed shore. At last I reached the Circus, just at the dawn of day. Oh, how I drank! how I reeled! how hungry I was! how thankful I was that I had so far at least escaped from the jaws of that howling wilderness. ... Just as I got clear of the bank of the creek, I heard a faint squeak, and looking about I saw, and immediately caught, a small dying wallaby, whose marsupial mother had evidently thrown it from her pouch. It only weighed about two ounces, and was scarcely furnished yet with fur. The instant I saw it, like an eagle I pounced upon it and ate it, living, raw, dying – fur, skin, bones, skull and all.

ERNEST GILES (1835-1897) come to Australia to work in the goldfields. After twice traversing the continent, in August 1873 he set off on an expedition into what was later to be named the Gibson Desert,

Ascent of the famous Ayers Rock, some 448 kilometres/278 miles southwest of Alice Springs. Its smooth slopes make it none too easy for visitors to climb.

The Olgas (Kata Tjuta), three dozen domed rocks near Ayers Rock, at dawn and at dusk.

west of the Petermann Range, in Western Australia. Giles' companion, Alfred Gibson, perished en route; Giles continued, carrying a forty-five pound/twenty kilogram keg of water on his shoulders for sixty miles/one hundred kilometres.

Keeping the Peace

The shearers, nine in number, have a cook of their own and buy their own extra rations, everything expect flour, beef, tea and sugar. They pay a man about £ 2 a week to cook for them while they are shearing. Christmas Eve, yesterday, was signalized by a chase and capture on the station. One of the shepherds came in the night before and said that his hut, which is near the road, had been robbed, while he was out with his sheep, and his blankets, clothes and rations stolen. Biddulph gave him some more blankets. Yesterday afternoon Julian came in in a state of great excitement to say that the man who had stolen the things had just passed the station, and that the shepherd had recognized the blankets he was carrying.

Biddulph mounted Julian's horse and went off through the bush at a gallop. Pat, Mr. Palmer's man, followed, also on horse-back, and everybody else on the station ran.

Biddulph presently came back with the culprit mounted on Pat's horse. He conducted him up to the stockyard, and the whole of the property was found in his possession. Moreover, he had borrowed Pat's horse the day before, promising to leave it at Exmoor, where he said his own horse was left, and then had ridden it on past the station evidently with the intention of stealing it.

Biddulph said he could not have the trouble and expense of sending him to Port Denison in custody, 110 miles, and afterwards appearing against him at Rockhampton, 370 miles off. So he had him then and there tied up to a tree and soundly flogged. Pat, who is a stout Irishman, being the executioner; and he bestowed two dozen with hearty goodwill, stimulated by the remembrance of his wrongs about the horse.

Justice being administered in this summary manner, Biddulph gave the man some rations that he might not be obliged to rob any more shepherds at stations and sent him off, at the same time warning the shepherds all down the road to look after their huts.

This description of Australian-style justice was written by RACHEL BIDDULPH HENNING (1826-1914) who arrived in Australia in 1854.

Paradise Lost

Even in my own life she was a scented land. In spring the bush used to be a constant choir of song; wings were everywhere; throughout the changing years might be heard the continual flying of birds: curlews, plovers, travelling duck, swans, wandering owls, bitterns, night-jars, and in the swamp the bleat of the snipe. From twenty directions at once you could hear the mopoke; from a hundred the curlew. There were the birds of all seasons, and the birds of the different hours of the day; there were the waders, the runners, the creepers, the carrion-eaters, the killers (kestrels, falcons, eagles), and those like the fantails that caught the fluttering insect on the wing.

In sheltered places where the blue wren was plentiful, he was literally in hundreds, a family flight being like a small jewelled cloud slipping tenuously through the undergrowth. In every bush I dare affirm there was a pigeon or a dove; the grass was a moving mass of parrots and parrakeets; while the trees glistened white with cockatoo, or were flamingo-pink with the galah.

Ants swarmed on the earth and trees; native bees, flies, gnats, beetles, spiders, and butterflies, burst from egg; rose from larvae, emerged from chrysalis. Everywhere things crept, swarmed, climbed, hummed, chirped, whistled, croaked, sang, and flowered. The air was full of the scent of life and honey, of the warm rich smell of feathers and fur. ...

There were no bad smells about the bush when the kingdom of the wild was its only kingdom; for the army of the small ate corruption before corruption became malodorous. It was not till the settlement came that the earth stank, and sewers burst. Once Australia smelt like the Spice Islands; the winds stooped as they passed because of her blossom; ships knew her before they came to her.

"We are near Australia," said the seamen. "Can't you smell the flowers?"

And people raised their heads and breathed in perfumes as it were out of heaven, for the land was still invisible, or but a bank low down on the horizon. Now only at the Leeuwin, as ships pass, do people raise their heads and snuff the air for scented winds. And then only for a short time in the year. Soon that, too, will be gone.

"It was a land of flowers!" said my grandmother. "At sea we smelt the rich scent of the country, different from anything we had ever known. We noticed the perfume long before we came to it. Those who had come home from Australia told us of it, and all who went out to Australia looked for it."

Outback bush country in the vicinity of Fitzroy Crossing. In many parts of Western Australia, no water is available for hundreds of miles.

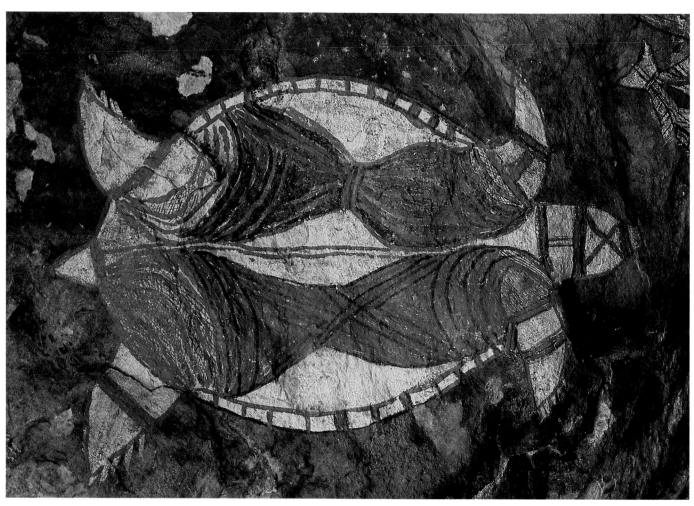

So spoke all the grandmothers. But who has said it in the full rich way that makes it live? Has anyone really sung to the world the song of this Scented Land? The thick-nosed and dull-eared derided her and we accepted their derision. They called her a land of songless birds and scentless flowers. The world believed them; and we for a century followed in the train of the world, even though on our breath her perfumes hung rich.

Indignantly I used to combat the statement:

"But our flowers *are* scented and our birds *do* sing!" I would counter.

"Oh, but your flowers do not smell like *English* flowers, and there are no *nightingales!*" would be the reply. Well, the rose, the lilac, and the nightingale are all Persian. As for our Australian wattle, London now calls it French mimosa. ...

"She was a scented land..." And only the exile knew her.

The Australian-born author DAME MARY GILMORE (1864-1962) worked as a teacher in many parts of Australia. She was also a vigorous campaigner for improved social services. In 1937 she was recognized by the Australian government for her community activities and literary achievements.

The Daughters of Eve

We sat in our navy blue serge tunics with white blouses. We sat without moving, our hands on our heads, our feet squarely on the floor under our desks.

The teacher read us a story: A girl got lost in the bush. She wandered all day looking for the way back home. When night fell she took refuge in a cave and fell asleep on the rocky floor. When she awoke she saw to her dismay that a snake had come while she slept and had coiled itself on her warm lap, where is now rested peacefully. The girl did not scream or move lest the snake be aroused and bite her. She stayed still without budging the whole day and the following night, until at last the snake slid away of its own accord. The girl was shocked but unharmed.

We sat on the floor of the gym in our gym uniforms; brown shirts and old-fashioned flared shorts no higher than six inches above the knee, beige ankle socks and brown sneakers. Our mothers had embroidered our initials in gold on the shirt pocket. We sat cross-legged in rows, our backs straight. ...

The gym mistress, in ballet slippers, stood before us, her hands clasped before her, her back straight,

...the paintings in red-brown hues, and black and white, have been repeatedly painted over in the course of centuries. They are incorporated into sacred sites that today con-[t]ue to hold a special significance for the contin-[e]nt's original inhabitants.

her stomach muscles firm. She said: If ever a snake should bite you, do not panic. Take a belt or a piece of string and tie a tourniquet around the affected limb between the bite and the heart. Take a sharp knife or razor blade. Make a series of cuts, criss-cross, over the bite. Then, suck at the cuts to remove the poison. Do not swallow. Spit out the blood and the poison. If you have a cut on you gum or lip, get a friend to suck out the poison instead. Then go to the nearest doctor. Try to kill the snake and take it with you. Otherwise, note carefully its distinguishing features. ...

I know of a girl who went bushwalking and sat on a snake curled up on a rock in the sun. The snake bit her. But since she was with a group that included boys, she was too embarrassed to say anything. So she kept on walking, until the poison overcame her. She fell ill and only then did she admit that a snake had bitten her on a very private part. But is was too late to help her. She died.

When I was sixteen my mother encouraged me to telephone a boy and ask him to be my partner for the school dance. She said: You are old enough to decide who you want to go out with and who you don't want to go out with. I trust you completely. After that I went out with a Roman Catholic, then an immigrant Dutchman, then an Indonesian.

My mother asked me what I thought I was doing. She said: You can go out with anyone you like as long as it's someone nice.

In the museum were two photographs. In the first, a snake had bitten and killed a young goat. In the second, the snake's jaws were stretched open and the goat was half inside the snake. The outline of the goat's body was visible within the body of the snake. The caption read: Snake trying to eat goat. Once snake begins to eat, it cannot stop. Jaws work like conveyor belt. ...

I encountered my first snake when I went for an early morning walk beside a wheat field in France. I walked gazing at the sky. When I felt a movement on my leg I looked down. Across my instep rested the tail of a tweedy-skinned snake. The rest of its body was inside the leg of my jeans, resting against my own bare leg. The head was at my knee.

I broke the rules. I screamed and kicked and stamped. The snake fell out of my jeans in a heap and fled into the wheat. I ran back to the house crying.

My friend said: "Did it offer you an apple?"

GLENDA ADAMS was born in Sydney in 1940. Like many of her stories, the extracts above portray some childhood experiences in Australia.

Homeward Bound

Cycad Valley is a National Park – though well protected from the public – where there are a unique species of cabbage-palm and ancient stands of Native Pine. The Horn River runs through its gorge: Limpy's Dreaming, the Native Cat, ran straight down the middle of the stream-bed. The Native Cat, or Tjilpa, is not a real cat but a small marsupial *(Dasyurus geoffreyi)* with outsize whiskers and an banded tail held vertically above its back. It may, sadly, be extinct.

There is a story that a young Tjilpa Ancestor, somewhere north of the MacDonnell Ranges, watched two eagle feathers fall from the sky and wanted to know where they came from. Following the Milky Way over the sandhills, he gradually attracted other Tjilpa Men, who joined the troop. On and on they went. Their fur was ruffled in the winter wind and their paws were cracked by the cold.

At last they reached the sea at Port Augusta and there, standing in the sea, was a pole so tall it touched the sky (like Dante's Mountain of Purgatory). Its top was white with sky-feathers and its lower half white with sea-feathers. The Tjilpa Men laid the pole on its side and carried it to Central Australia.

Limpy had never come here because of some long-standing feud. But he had recently heard over the bush telegraph that three of his distant relatives were living there – or, rather, dying there, alongside their tjuringa storehouse. He wanted to see them before they went.

We drove for seven hours, from seven until two. Limpy sat in front between the driver and Marian, motionless but for a quick dart of the eyes to right or to left. …

We drove for almost an hour; the road twisted through the purple cliffs. There were gigantic boulders smeared with black streaks, and the cycads, like magnified tree ferns, sprang up between them. The day was stifling.

Then the river vanished underground, leaving on the surface a stagnant pool with reedy margins. A purple heron flew off and settled in a tree. The road had come to an end.

We got out and followed Limpy along a well-worn footpath which threaded round the rocks and the water and came out into a basin of dark-red rock with receding layers of strata, reminding one of the seats in a Greek theatre. There was the usual tin shack under a tree. …

As I wrote in my notebooks, the mystics believe the ideal man shall walk himself to a 'right death'. He who has arrived 'goes back'.

In Aboriginal Australia, there are specific rules for 'going back' or, rather, for singing your way to where you belong: to your 'conception site', to the place where your tjuringa is stored. Only then can you become – or re-become – the Ancestor. The concept is quite similar to Heraclitus's mysterious dictum, 'Mortals and immortals, alive in their death, dead in each other's life.'

Limpy hobbled ahead. We followed on tiptoe. The sky was incandescent, and sharp shadows fell cross the path. A trickle of water dribbled down the cliff.

'Tjuringa place up there!' said Limpy, softly, pointing to a dark cleft high above our heads.

In a clearing there were three 'hospital' bedsteads, with mesh springs and no mattresses, and on them lay the three dying men. They were almost skeletons. Their beards and hair had gone. One was strong enough to lift an arm, another to say something. When they heard who Limpy was, all three smiled, spontaneously, the same toothless grin.

Arkady folded his arms, and watched.

'Aren't they wonderful?' Marian whispered, putting her hand in mine and giving it a squeeze.

Yes. They were all right. They knew where they were going, smiling at death in the shade of a ghost-gum.

"Songlines", by BRUCE CHATWIN (1940-1989) is regarded as the modern traveller's 'bible' to Australia. Chatwin's texts often explore the richness and complexity of the Aboriginal culture.

The Aborigines of Sydney

Most of the aborigines of these parts were exterminated, by imported disease or by brute force, within a few decades of the first white settlement. Yet two centuries later a few hundred cling to their roots in Sydney, at the very site of the European coming. They are called 'coories' here, and like the water of the harbour, like the exotic foliage of the parks and headlands, they are a reminder of stranger, older things than Kev and his kind can conceive. To some Australians the aborigines are a blot on the conscience, to others just a pain in the neck: still, in the

igures carved and painted by the Aborigines, as here in Darwin, are sold to tourists as souvenirs.

The Twelve Apostles, southwest of Melbourne, have been carved out of the steep cliffs by the movement of seawater.

A young opal-prospecting couple in Coober Pedy. In the middle of the South Australian desert, prospectors live in dugouts in order to protect themselves from the scorching heat.

end most people thought the coories were worth feeling sorry for, and feel sorry for them I did.

Though their community has produced some celebrities in its time, notably boxers, they live mostly in more luckless quarters of the town, and do not show much as a rule. As it chanced, however, while I was in Sydney this time they celebrated Aboriginal Day. The aboriginal flag of gold, black and yellow flew, to the consternation of Old Australians, side by side with the national flag on Sydney Town Hall, and a march through town was announced, to be followed by a rally at Alexandria Park. Alas, all this went sadly awry. Nobody seemed to know where the march was to begin, or when, somebody pulled the flag down from the Town Hall, not everyone seemed to have mastered the rally chant – *What do we want? Land rights! What have we got? Bugger all!* – and the arrangements ran so late that when the time came for speeches everyone had gone home. 'They are a *random* people,' was the convincing explanation I was given, when I asked if this was true to coorie form.

By the time I reached Alexandria Park Aboriginal Day seemed to have fizzled out altogether, and all I found was a small huddle of dark-skinned people around an open bonfire, surrounded by litter on the edge of the green. They greeted me with a wan concern, offering me beer out of a ice-bucket, sidling around me rather, and occasionally winking. A small thin boy with cotton wool stuffed in one ear wandered here and there leading a black puppy on a string. Others kicked a football about in the gathering dusk, and around the fire a handful of older men and women looked sadly into the flames. A strong smell of alcohol hung over us, and the man with the bucket urged me quietly, again and again, to have one for the road, dear. Had the rally been a success? I asked. 'Yeah,' they said, and looked into the fire.

I *did* feel sorry for them. They were like last wasted survivors from some primeval holocaust, whose memories of their own civilization were aeons ago expunged. Did they have a Sydney all their own, I wondered, long ago near the beginnings of time? Did their flag fly braver then? When I said goodbye and drove away ('Go on, dear, just one') the lights of the downtown tower blocks were shining in the distance: but in the shadows at the edge of the park the bonfire flames were dancing still, and the frail figures of the indigenes moved unsteadily in the flicker.

The Welsh traveller JAN MORRIS (b. 1926) has travelled and written about almost every part of the world.

An angler in the vicinity of Roeburne on Australian's west coast, where loneliness and abundant fish are guaranteed.

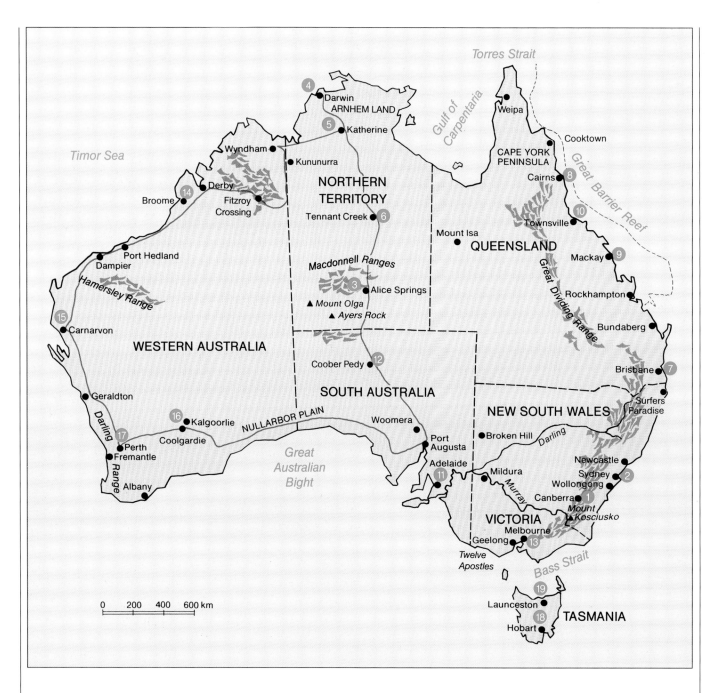

GENERAL INFORMATION

LOCATION. Australia lies in the southern hemisphere. It extends from the Indian to the Pacific Oceans between the 155th and 110th lines of longitude and between the 10th and 44th lines of latitude. Around forty percent of the country is situated north of the Tropic of Capricorn and therefore, in the tropics. The name Australia derives from the Latin "terra australis incognita", meaning "unknown south land".

SIZE. With an area of 7,686,300 square kilometres/2,967,680 square miles,

Australia is the world's smallest continent and is comparable with the area of the continental United States not including Alaska (7,704,000 square kilometres/2,974,514 square miles). It extends for some 3,700 kilometres/2,300 miles from north to south, and when including the island of Tasmania, for some 4,000 kilometres/2,485 miles. From east to west, Australia also measures 4,000 kilometres. Australia's coastal perimeter stretches for more than 20,000 kilometres/12,000 miles. The country is divided topographically into three large regions: the West Australian tableland, comprising around one half of the coun-

try, the interior tableland and the Great Dividing Range, which extends from the northern end of the Pacific Coast down as far as Tasmania.

INHABITANTS. With a total of some 16.8 million inhabitants, Australia has a population density of two persons per square kilometre/one-third of a square mile; in comparison, Great Britain has a density of 236 persons per square kilometre. Around eighty percent live in large urban areas, while more than one-half of the continent's inhabitants live in the four cities of Sydney, Melbourne, Brisbane and Perth. The 160,000 original inhabitants (of which 60,000 are pure Aborigines) make up not quite one percent of the population.

CLIMATE. Australia is not referred to as being "down under" without reason. It is not only situated on the diametrically opposite side of the globe but also its seasons are the opposite of Europe's: while Europeans are enduring winter, Australia's residents experience summer. In the north part of the continent summer is hot, tropically humid and accompanied by heavy rainfall while winters are mild. In the south the climate is warm and dry in the summer and moderate during the winters.

CLIMATIC TABLE. Below are listed the maximum and minimum average monthly temperatures in Centigrade as well as the average precipitation in millimetres.

guage has been further enriched by Aboriginal words, such as "boomerang".

MONEY AND CURRENCY. Australian Dollar ($A). The Australian Dollar is equal to approximately 40 British pence or 70 US cents. Prices in Australia are comparable with those in the United Kingdom. The usual credit cards are accepted everywhere in the cities and are required for car rentals.

ENTRY REQUIREMENTS. A visa is required for entry to Australia in addition to a valid passport. Visas can be obtained free of charge from the Australian High Commission, Australia House, The Strand, London WC2 B4LA, United Kingdom and from the Australian Consulate-General, International Building, 630 Fifth Avenue, New York, 10111, USA. Several weeks are required for processing.

AUSTRALIAN TOURIST AUTHORITY IN THE UK
Australian Tourist Commission, Gemini House, 10-18 Putney Hill, Putney, London SW 15, Tel.: (081) 78 02 227.

AUSTRALIAN TOURIST AUTHORITIES IN THE USA
Australian Tourist Commission, 489 Fifth Avenue, 31st Floor, New York, New York 10017, Tel.: (212) 687-6300.
Australian Tourist Commission, 2121 Avenue of the Stars, Suite 1200, Los Angeles, California 90067, Tel.: (213) 552-1988.

TOURIST OFFICES IN AUSTRALIA
Australian Tourist Commission, 80 William Street, Woolloomooloo, Sydney, NSW 2011, Tel.: (02) 360 11 11 (for Australia in general)
Canberra Tourism Development Bureau, Northbourne Avenue, Canberra, ACT 2600, Tel.: (062) 45 64 64.
Northern Territory Government Tourist Bureau, Ford Plaza Building, Todd Mall, Alice Springs, NT 0870, Tel.: (089) 52 12 99.
Queensland Tourist & Travel Corporation, 123 Eagle Street, Brisbane, QLD 4000, Tel.: (07) 833 54 00.
Tourism South Australia, 18 King William Street, Adelaide, SA 5000, Tel.: (08) 210 72 00.
Tourism Tasmania, Franklin Wharf, Hobart, TAS 7000, Tel.: (002) 30 02 11.
New South Wales Tourism Commission, 140 Phillip Street, Sydney, NSW 2000, Tel.: (02) 231 71 00.
Western Australia Tourism Commission, 16 St. Georges Terrace, Perth, WA 6000, Tel.: (09) 220 17 00.
Victorian Tourism Commission, World Trade Centre, Melbourne, VIC 3005, Tel.: (03) 619 94 44.

		Jan.	Feb.	Mar.	Apr.	May	June	July	Aug.	Sept.	Oct.	Nov.	Dec.
Sydney	Max.	26	25	25	22	19	17	16	17	20	22	24	25
	Min.	18	18	17	15	11	9	8	9	11	13	15	17
	mm	98	113	128	127	124	131	105	81	70	75	78	80
Melbourne	Max.	26	26	24	20	17	14	13	15	17	20	22	24
	Min.	14	14	13	11	9	7	6	6	8	9	11	13
	mm	48	50	54	59	57	50	48	49	58	67	59	58
Perth	Max.	30	30	28	24	21	18	17	18	19	21	25	27
	Min.	18	18	17	14	12	10	9	9	10	11	14	16
	mm	8	11	20	40	124	186	174	139	81	55	21	14
Darwin	Max.	32	32	32	33	32	31	30	31	33	34	34	33
	Min.	25	25	25	24	22	20	20	21	23	25	25	25
	mm	391	330	260	103	14	3	1	2	13	50	126	243
Alice Springs	Max.	37	36	33	29	23	20	19	22	26	31	34	35
	Min.	22	21	18	14	9	6	4	7	10	15	18	20
	mm	34	39	22	12	17	16	13	12	6	20	23	32

TIME ZONES. Australia has three time zones: Eastern Standard Time (EST) is thirty minutes ahead of Central Standard Time (CST), which in turn is two hours ahead of Western Standard Time (WST). During the summer months from October to March, clocks and watches are put forward one hour.

LANGUAGE. The official language of Australia is English. However, apart from variations in pronunciation, neologisms and words formed from others blended together have all become standard features of Australian English. The lan-

INOCULATIONS. No vaccinations are required if visitors are travelling from Europe.

CUSTOMS. All items of personal use as well as one litre of alcohol and two hundred cigarettes may be imported to Australia without duty charges being levelled. There are no restrictions on the importation of Australian currency. However, it is forbidden to import foodstuffs, fruit, plants, seeds and animals, or to carry these items from one state to another. Pets brought to the country must be held in quarantine for six months.

UNITED KINGDOM REPRESENTATION IN AUSTRALIA
British High Commission, Commonwealth Avenue, Yarralumla, Canberra, ACT 2600, Tel.: (61) (62) 70 66 66.

Local tourist information is provided in the individual towns or at the points of interest as indicated below. Each state and territory has travel centres in its capital city; these centres will book tours, accommodation and transport.

TRANSPORT

AIR. Flights to Australia from Europe require between twenty and twenty-four hours, depending on the route and re-fuelling stops. Planes of Australia's Quantas Airline refuel in Thailand's capital Bangkok. Most other airlines also take the eastern route, flying to Australia via Thailand or Singapore. Many airlines offer attractive holiday tariffs. Reduced-price scheduled flights (IT tariffs) can be obtained only in conjunction with hotel reservations. Most international flights terminate in Sydney. There are, however, connecting flights available to Perth, Melbourne, Brisbane, Cairns, Adelaide, Townsville and Darwin.
Australian Airlines and Ansett are the two major domestic carriers. Most reduced flight tickets, for example the See Australia Fare, must be purchased in the visitor's home country before arrival in Australia. Information may be obtained from the airline branches:
Quantas Airways, 182 The Strand, London WC2, Tel.: (081) 846 0321/2/3; or Quantas Airways Ticket Office, 542 Fifth Avenue, New York, New York 10036; Reservations: 1000 Cherry Ave., Suite 225, San Bruno, California 94066, Tel.: (toll free) 800-227-4500.

RAIL. Journeys can last between twelve and sixty-five hours. The most important trains are:
From Sydney: Indian Pacific (to Perth), The Alice (to Alice Springs), Melbourne Express and Inter Capital Daylight Express (to Melbourne) and Brisbane Limited Express (to Brisbane).
From Adelaide: Trans Australian (to Perth), The Ghan (Alice Springs).
From Melbourne: Sydney Express (to Sydney), The Overland (to Adelaide).
From Brisbane: The Sunlander and The Queenslander (to Cairns).
Austrailtickets allow unlimited travel by rail. The passes are valid for periods between two weeks and three months, with prices varying accordingly; they must be purchased abroad. Information and reservations are available from British and American agents of the Australian Railway Tourland Agency as well as from most larger travel agencies.

SHIPS, FERRIES. Numerous promoters offer cruises to Australia. Those travellers

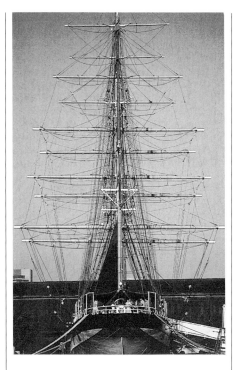

In Melbourne's harbour.

not wishing to cover the entire distance from Europe to Australia on board ship can fly from Europe to Asia, Bali or the Fiji Islands and embark from there for Australia.
In Australia itself, there are three sailings per week from Melbourne to Devonport in Tasmania. Australia's many lakes, islands and several larger rivers make it well suited to those wishing to travel by boat. Houseboats can be rented on the Hawkesbury River, north of Sydney, and on the Murray River. Charter boats, motorized yachts and sailing craft are available on all coasts.

CAR AND CARAVAN HIRE. Caravans can be rented in almost every town. A valid driving licence is required; an international driving licence is recognized everywhere. The driver must be at least twenty-one to twenty-five years of age, depending on the hiring company.
Hire charges range between $A 68 to 90, depending on the size of the vehicle. Arrangements can be made for the vehicle to be left at the intended destination.

BUSES. Express buses offer a good value alternative to domestic flights. Pioneer Express, Bus Australia and Greyhound as well as smaller regional companies provide services throughout the country,

offering various special arrangements. Tickets should be reserved before the start of a journey. Some special offers are only valid when booked from outside Australia.

ACCOMMODATION

CAMPING SITES. Australia is ideally suited for camping. There are camping sites not only in the vicinity of all large towns but even in the most remote corners of the country. Some sites offer caravans or cabins for hire. Camping in the open countryside is generally allowed in Australia. However, one should not venture out too far into the bush, and, if camping alone in a national park, it is best to first inform the ranger station.

HOTELS. In Australia there are hotels in all price categories. These range from small family establishments, charging $A 15 per room without bath, to houses offering bed-and-breakfast, and the international hotel chains such as Regent, Hyatt and Hilton. A number of Australian hotels groups cooperate in offering hotel vouchers providing accommodation packages at an inclusive price.

MOTELS. Motels are also available throughout the country. As a rule, they include a separate shower and toilet as well as a television, telephone and fridge. Their prices begin around $A 25.

APARTMENTS. are available in the larger holiday areas, for example in Cairns. Most are fully equipped. Choices range from simple two room apartments to luxury villas.

YOUTH HOSTELS. Some one-hundred-thirty youth hostels are available at an average of $A 9.50 per night. For those without a youth hostel card the price is higher. The youth hostels face stiff competition from the Backpacker Association, which also offers cheap accommodation in multi-bed rooms (from $A 10 per night). There are also YMCAs, which are open to non-members.

FOOD AND DRINK

The European and Asiatic origins of the population are reflected in the national

Old railway tracks dating from the gold-rush days in the vicinity of Broome (WA).

cuisine. The warm climate allows all conceivable fruits to thrive, while fishing provides all manners of seafood from trout to oysters and lobster. National dishes such as beef are served in many variations and one should try such specialities as Sydney rock oyster and Morton Bay bug. Also to be recommended is a rack of lamb (roasted lamb ribs glazed with honey), filet of beef filled with oysters, and kangaroo-, buffalo- or crocodile-steaks.

Australia is a nation of beer-drinkers and the rich diversity of beers on offer is hardly surpassed in any European country. However, the Australian wine industry has been gaining a good reputation in recent years; the grapes thrive in the Australian sunshine. The more known wine-producing regions are Barossa Valley (South Australia), and Hunter Valley (New South Wales). Both have, in part, been built up on German wine-making traditions.

Alcohol is bought in special "Bottle Shops". Beer is the most popular drink in the pubs. Pubs are open throughout the day, closing around 10 or 11 p.m. Not every restaurant has a licence to serve alcohol. Those not wishing to go without beer or wine during the meal should look for the notice "BYO" at the entrance to the restaurant: these initials stand for "Bring Your Own", inviting diners to bring a bottle of whatever their favourite drink may happen to be.

SHOPPING TIPS

Opals are often on offer in a great variety of hues, ranging from turquoise-green to dark blue. Other popular souvenirs are Aboriginal handcrafts, mainly decorated boomerangs or all sorts of leather goods, from bags to leather dresses and hats.

POINTS OF INTEREST

Circled numbers refer to the map on page 48; italicized numbers refer to colour photographs.

Listed according to state.

AUSTRALIAN CAPITAL TERRITORY (ACT)

CANBERRA ①. Australia's capital (298,000 residents) occupies its own Capital Territory of around 2,360 square kilometres/910 square miles. The city first came into existence during this century and has been generously provided with artificial lakes, parks and green areas. Two hills, Capital Hill and City Hill, are situated at the centre of the city. The *Canberra Planning Exhibition* in Commonwealth Park uses films and models to explain how the capital has developed (open daily, 9 a.m. to 5 p.m.). The First World War *War Memorial* (Limestone Avenue) houses a display of weapons, flags, war photographs and even a Japanese submarine (open daily, 9 a.m. to 5 p.m.).

Parliament House (King George Terrace) stands atop Capital Hill. Opened in 1988, it contains a café, theatre and exhibition rooms (open daily, 9 a.m. to 5 p.m.). Immediately next to it, the old *Parliament House* may also be visited (open daily, 9 a.m. to 5 p.m.).

Also of interest, owing primarily to its architecture, is the *High Court of Australia*, situated on the south bank of Lake Burley Griffin. By way of a bridge, visitors can reach the *Australian National Gallery;* its eleven sections exhibit some seventy thousand works by Australian as well as foreign artists. From behind the reinforced glass at the *Royal Australian Mint* (Denison Street), visitors can watch money being minted. An exhibition of coins documents the history of currency (open Monday to Friday, 9 a.m. to 4 p.m.). It is worth making a detour to *Embassy Row*. Many of the embassies here have been built in a style appropriate to the country they represent, thereby providing a colourful mixture of the architecture of different nations. Information is available from the Canberra Tourist Bureau, Jolimont Centre, Northbourne Avenue/Alinga Street.

NEW SOUTH WALES (NSW)

SYDNEY ②. The capital of New South Wales (3.6 million residents) is not only the oldest and largest city in Australia but it also epitomizes the fifth continent, just as its Opera House has become an urban Australian landmark. Sydney's enormous natural harbour encouraged the first settlement here, from which exploration of the continent could be undertaken. Sydney serves as a focal point for Australia's commercial, industrial and cultural activities. The *Opera House*, roofed with the famous sail-like construction, stands on the Bennelong Point peninsula, not far from Circular Quay. From the Opera House, there are good views of the *Sydney Harbour Bridge*. With a central span of over 500 metres/1,640 feet, and with a length of over 1,000 metres/3,280 feet, the bridge ranks among the largest single-span bridges in the world. Trips around the harbour can be made from Circular Quay, or, aboard a hydrofoil, one can quickly cross over to those districts lying on the other bank and to the bathing beach of Manly. From Circular Quay, both George Street and Pitt Street lead to the city centre with its multi-storey office buildings. However, beyond its commercial centre, Sydney consists of countless detached and semi-detached houses and their small gardens. The city is so spread out that it can take up to half a day to drive across it. An interesting district in Sydney is *The Rocks,* the oldest part of the town. It is on the west bank of the ferry port and has been restored in recent years. *The Rocks Visitors Centre* (George Street) displays documents and films relating to the history of the district. *Cadman's Cottage* (George Street) was built in 1816 and is Sydney's oldest residence. Nowadays it houses a small exhibition. Only a few streets further on and higher up is *Observatory Park* (Argyle/Kent Street). The observatory, dating from 1857, can be viewed if prior notice is given. From the forty-eighth floor of the *Australia Square Tower* (George/Hunter Street) good views of the city and harbour can be enjoyed.

The skyline of Sydney.

The *Australian Museum* provides insights into the natural world and its development. It houses one of Australia's largest natural history collections of flora and fauna (College Street, Tuesday to Saturday, 10 a.m. to 5 p.m.; Sunday and Monday, 12 noon to 5 p.m.). The wide variety of flora growing in the *Royal Botanic Gardens* (Macquarie Street) also provides instructive insights into natural history. Those who enjoy the hustle and bustle of big cities and the world of high class retail sales should make straight for the restored *Queen Victoria Building* (George Street). The more than two hundred outlets on the several storeys of this exclusive shopping centre offer luxury articles produced in Australia as well as interna-

tional fashion and jewellery. *Chinatown,* with its Chinese restaurants and markets, and Paddington, the former working-class quarter where nowadays boutiques, antique shops and art galleries are to be found both have extra-special atmospheres. However, to escape all this excitement, there are excursions to be made into the area around Sydney. The *Blue Mountains* lie only eighty kilometres/fifty miles to the west and offer fascinating mountain scenery with gorges, waterfalls and vast eucalyptus forests. Boat excursions or a rented houseboat enable visitors to take in the countryside bordering the *Hawkesbury River* (thirty kilometres/nineteen miles from Sydney). This area is most popular due to its attractive palm trees and giant ferns. Information is available from the New South Wales Tourist Commission (see Information). *6/7, 9, 10, 11, 13*

NORTHERN TERRITORY (NT)

ALICE SPRINGS ③. With its 23,000 residents, Alice lies at the centre of the continent, "the red heart" of Australia. The town was founded in 1872 when a telegraph line was laid from Adelaide to the north in order to create a connection to England via the underwater cable from Darwin. Nowadays, the *Old Telegraph Station* can be viewed three kilometres/two miles north of the town (open daily, 10 a.m. to 4 p.m.). The *Old Stuart Gaol* (1907) is one of Alice Springs' oldest buildings.

At the *School of the Air* (Head Street), visitors can listen to teachers instructing

the children of the outback farmsteads by means of two-way radio. An exhibition at the *Frontier Camel Farm* (Ross Highway) illustrates the exploration of the Northern Territory, in which camels played an important part. Excursions can be made, for example, to *Chateau Hornsby,* the only winery in central Australia (Stuart Highway). Those wishing to become better acquainted with "the red heart" of the continent will have to drive or fly from Alice to *Ayers Rock.* Information is available from the NT Government Tourist Bureau (also see Information). *4/5, 35*

This gigantic monolith fascinates every visitor to Australia. It is sacred to the Aborigines and was first visited by tourists in the 1930s; in the meantime more than 300,000 visitors from all over the world come here annually to climb to the top of the rock and to witness the natural spectacle of the rock glowing fiery red in the light of the setting sun. The *Yulara Resort,* built at some distance, provides accommodation and information for several thousand guests daily. Within sight of Uluru, as the Aborigines call the Rock, are *The Olgas,* a rock formation of more than thirty large domed rocks, which, like Ayers Rock, are many million years old and which rise up directly out of the vast expanse of the outback. *36/37*

DARWIN ④. Australia's northernmost port has 73,000 residents, making it the largest town in the Northern Territory. *The Chinese Temple* (Bennett Street) stands as an example of the town's cultural diversity. Government House, (Esplanade) with its fine view out over the harbour, was built in the style of the tropics. The *Museum of Arts and Sciences* (Conacher Street) exhibits Aboriginal handicrafts and exhibitions of modern Australian art and of indigenous animal life. *Kakadu National Park,* which can be reached via the Arnhem Land Highway, is situated 140 kilometres/87 miles east of Darwin. Some 250 bird and 75 reptile species have their habitat in the national park. The Aboriginal rock paintings are also of great interest, some of which are thought to be 20,000 years old. Park rangers conduct daily tours to the rock art at Obirr and Nourlangie Rock. Information is available from the Northern Territory

Government Tourist Bureau, 31 Smith Street Mall. *40, 41, 43*

KATHERINE ⑤. With more than 5,000 residents, Katherine is the third largest town in the Northern Territory. The *Mimi Aboriginal Arts and Crafts Centre* (Pearce Street) is well worth visiting. An interesting excursion can be made to the twelve kilometre/seven mile long Katherine Gorge, some thirty kilometres/ nineteen miles to the northeast. A boat trip provides the best means of viewing the unusual cliff formations carved out by the Katherine River. Information is available from the Northern Territory Government Tourist Bureau, Stuart Highway/Lindsay Avenue.

TENNENT CREEK ⑥. This small mining township actively produced gold and copper until 1980. The *Old Battery* (Peko Road, Monday to Friday, 9 a.m. to 3 p.m.) provides an insight into the craft of panning for gold, and a small museum relates the history of mining. Some fifteen kilometres/nine miles to the northwest, granite formations shaped by wind erosion, and suitably named the Devil's Marbles, rear up on either side of the Stuart Highway. Information is available from the Northern Territory Government Tourist Bureau, Paterson/Davidson Street.

QUEENSLAND (QLD)

BRISBANE ⑦. The capital of the "Sunshine State" has close to 1.3 million residents. Inside of *City Hall,* the "Tourism Brisbane" office provides general tourist information (King George Square, Monday to Friday, 9 a.m. to 3 p.m.). One of the city's oldest buildings is the *Old Windmill,* dating from 1829, which later housed Brisbane's fire alarm and served as a meteorological station. The *Queensland Cultural Centre* (Victoria Bridge) contains a museum, library and several art exhibitions. *17*

CAIRNS ⑧. This city in Queensland's far north has become a tourist centre on account of its beaches. However, in addition to its glorious sandy beaches, Cairns also boasts several museums, such as the *House of 10,000 Shells* and *Rusty's Market* (Grafton Street). A worthwhile excursion can be made to *Green*

Island, a coral island where at low tide, a diversity of colours and shapes can be viewed. In the museum, descriptions and explanations concerning the Great Barrier Reef are featured. Information is available from the Tourist Office, Sheridan/Alpin Street. *26/27*

MACKAY ⑨. This picturesque town (15,000 residents), with streets bordered by palms and attractive houses, is one of the largest ports for sugar-cane shipments in the world. Many tours to the *Great Barrier Reef* and the reef's islands start from here.
In *Queens Park* (East Gordon Street) many exotic plants may be seen as well as orchids growing under glass. Information is available from the Tourist Office, Nebo Road.

TOWNSVILLE ⑩. To the northwest of Brisbane is Townsville with its 109,000 residents. The *Great Barrier Reef Wonderland* located at the port (Flinders Street, open daily, 9.30 a.m. to 5 p.m.) offers a coral aquarium, while a panorama cinema provides a close-up view of the reef's submarine world. Excursions to the islands can be undertaken from here. Information is available from the Tourist Office, Flinders Street.

SOUTH AUSTRALIA (SA)

ADELAIDE ⑪. The capital of South Australia, situated between Gulf St. Vincent and Mount Lofty, was founded in 1836. The population of this metropolis, with its southern atmosphere, now

Above: On the coast near Darwin. Below: Festival Centre in Adelaide.

numbers around one million. The *Constitutional Museum* (North Terrace) relates the history of the state. *Ayers House* (North Terrace, Tuesday to Friday, 10 a.m. to 4 p.m.; Saturday/Sunday, 2 to 4 p.m.), the former residence of Prime Minister Henry Ayers, also displays its own history. Immediately beside the house is Rundle Mall, a pedestrian precinct with boutiques, cafés and restaurants. Fresh food items can be bought at the *Central Market* (Grote Street). Not far inland of Adelaide is the 770 metre/2,526 foot high Mount Lofty, much favoured by hang-gliding enthusiasts. An excursion to *Barossa Valley,* fifty kilometres/ thirty miles northeast of Adelaide, takes one into vineyards where German wine-making traditions continue. At Murray Bridge (eighty kilometres/fifty miles to the southeast), paddle-steamer excursions can be made and houseboats hired. Information is available from South Australian Government Travel Centre, 21 King William Street.

COOBER PEDY (12), some one thousand kilometres/six hundred miles northwest of Adelaide, has come into being amid inhospitable desert surroundings owing to its vast opal deposits (seventy-five percent of the world's opals are found here). The almost two thousand residents seek shelter from the heat, which can reach 50° Celsius/122°Fahrenheit, below ground in what are termed "dugouts"; even the settlement's church is subterranean. The prospectors are pleased to be watched at work, and a licence obtained from the Department of Mining and Energy allows anyone to prospect for the beautiful stones. *46*

HAHNDORF. The mountain settlement in the Barossa Valley, northeast of Adelaide, was founded by German immigrants in 1839. Many old buildings are still in existence, and traditional German shooting competitions and beer festivals continue to this day. The *Folk Museum* in the *Hahndorf Academy* (Princess Highway) displays exhibits illustrating German traditions as well as an exhibition of pictures by Hans Heysen (1877-1968), artist who won fame in Australia. Information is available from Tourist Information, 64 Main Road.

VICTORIA (VIC)

BALLARAT. The 1851 gold rush turned this sleepy sheepraising settlement to the west of Melbourne seemingly overnight into a township (59,000 residents today). The open air museum on *Sovereign Hill* (open daily, 9.30 a.m. to 5 p.m.), southeast of Ballarat, is an accurate reconstruction of a town at the time of the gold rush. Local inhabitants dressed in Victorian costume run the post office, bakery, printers and other shops in the museum village.

MELBOURNE (13). Some three million residents are at home in this commercial metropolis, Australia's second largest city after Sydney. From the *World Trade Centre* (Spencer/Flinders Street), visitors can look out over an expanse of houses

In the centre of Melbourne.

and over the trade fair centre by the Yarra River. Also close to the river is the *Victorian Arts Centre* (St. Kilda Road) with its art museum, opera performances and concerts. The terrace cafés in *City Square* (Swanston Street/Flinders Lane) beckon with the invitation of refreshments. At the *Royal Melbourne Zoo* in the district of Parkville, kangaroos, koalas and duck-billed platypuses live. An excursion to *Phillip Island* allows visitors to enjoy Australia's most entertaining animals. Every evening the fairy penguins can be watched returning from the sea to their nesting grounds. About one hour's drive from the city are the *Dangenong Ranges,* hilly countryside through which *Puffing Billy,* an eighty-year-old steam engine, makes its way on narrow-gauge tracks. The eucalyptus forests proliferate on the hills, which were in fact once active volcanoes. Farming communities have now become established in the valleys. *18, 19*

WESTERN AUSTRALIA (WA)

BROOME (14) fulfilled most of the global requirement of mother-of-pearl until cultured pearls reduced the demand. Broome's *Chinatown,* situated at the port, is a relic dating from the time when multitudes of Asians settled in the town, working as divers. Today, Broome, with its almost 3,000 residents, is active economically in the export of meat produced on the large cattle stations in the vast expanses of Australia's hinterland.

CARNARVON (15). Attractive sections of coastline, with steep cliffs and golden-brown sandy beaches, characterize this locality. Carnarvon, however, is best known for its satellite station. Some seventy kilometres/forty-three miles north of the town, the *Blowholes* on the coast provide a natural spectacle: the seawater is forced into holes in the cliffs causing fountains of water, up to twenty-five metres/eighty-two feet high, to be syphoned out at the other end.

FREMANTLE. Only twenty kilometres/twelve miles southwest of Perth, Fremantle is Australia's most important port on the Indian Ocean. Numerous old buildings dating from the time of first settlement (1829), such as the 1831 *Round House Gaol* line High Street. This twelve-sided prison now houses a historical museum (open daily, 10 a.m. to 5 p.m.). In *War Memorial Park* is Monument Hill, the highest point in Fremantle, with memorials to those who fell in World War II. Information is available from the Tourist Bureau, Town Hall, Adelaide/William Street.

KALGOORLY (16). This town, today with 24,000 residents, became famous at the turn of the century following the discovery of gold in 1893. The *Golden Mile Museum* (Egan Street) is devoted to this period. A visit can be made to the *Hainauld Gold Mine* (Boulder Block Road), where visitors are taken down as far as sixty metres/two hundred feet below ground. Information is available from the Tourist Bureau, Hannan Street.

PERTH ⑰. The capital of Western Australia, with 1.1 million residents, is situated in the southwest of the continent directly on the Indian Ocean.

During a tour of the city, visitors will certainly be impressed by *Government House* (St. George's Terrace) which serves as the official residence of the Governor of Western Australia. The former town hall (Barrack/Hay Street) was built in 1870, but now all that remains is the town-hall tower nestled between modern façades.

Still standing, however, is the *Old Court House* (Terrace Road), built in 1836.

Just outside the city, visitors can relax in the four hundred hectares/nine-hundred-ninety acres of the large botanical gardens of King's Park. Here, there are flowers, trees and various animals as well as sports grounds, memorials and picnic sites. The *Old Mill* at the southern end of the Narrow Bridge is the oldest of Perth's town's mills; it now houses exhibits from the colonial period (open daily, except Tuesday and Friday, 1 to 3 p.m.).

There are other interesting museums in the town. Information is available from the Western Australia Government Travel Centre, Hay/King Street.

TASMANIA (TAS)

HOBART ⑱. The capital of this island off the southeast coast of Australia has close to 180,000 residents and is the economic and cultural centre of Tasmania, which after the Australian Capital Territory is the second smallest federal state on the continent. The *Tasmanian Museum and Art Gallery* (Argyle Street, open daily, 10 a.m. to 5 p.m.) documents the history of Hobart's settlement. Close by is the *Cat and Fiddle Arcade* (Murray Street) with its great variety of shops. Here, it is well worth visiting *Jewels*, where precious stones are cut. The *Anglesea Barracks* (Davey Street) is one of the oldest such barracks in Australia, constructed in 1811. A tour through the Hobart district of Battery Point allows visitors to view the lovingly restored buildings. An excursion can be made to the ruins of a convict colony (1830-1877) situated on a promontory some one hundred kilometres/sixty miles to the south. A guided tour through sections of the prison building provides an insight into

Above: Koala bears. Below: Kangaroos.

the prison existence led by criminals in the nineteenth century. The sea park is also of interest: fish, penguins, sea-lions and pelicans can be observed.

LAUNCESTON ⑲. Agriculture and the textile industry have determined the character of this town of 91,000 residents, situated about two hundred kilometres/one-hundred twenty miles north of Hobart. The *Queen Victoria Museum* (Wellington Street, Monday to Saturday, 10 a.m. to 5 p.m.; Sunday, 2 to 5 p.m.) exhibits the island's flora and fauna, minerals and Aboriginal art. The planetarium displays the constellations visible in the night skies over the

southern hemisphere. About two kilometres/one mile from the centre of town, the South Esk River has carved out the deep *Cataract Gorge,* which can be crossed on a chair lift. Information is available from the Tourist Bureau, St. John/Peterson Street.

QUEENSTOWN. This small town's *Gallery* (Sticht/Driffilt Street, Monday to Friday, 10 a.m. to 4 p.m.; Saturday/Sunday, 1 to 4 p.m.) displays a comprehensive collection of over one thousand photographs detailing the settlement of Tasmania's west coast. Information is available from the Tourist Bureau, 39 Orr Street.

ST. HELENS. This bathing resort at the northeastern end of the island is known for its sandy beaches and water-sport facilities. *St. Helens Point,* at the end of a promontory, provides fine views along the coastline. Close by is the *Mount William National Park* with its large eucalyptus forests.

NATIONAL PARKS

(A selection from the more than 2,000 national parks in Australia.)

BUNYA MOUNTAINS NATIONAL PARK: QLD, 300 kilometres/180 miles northwest of Brisbane. Mountain rain forest with giant bunya pines, eucalyptus forests and waterfalls, king parrots. Open: December to February. Information centre, camping, accommodation, walking.

FLINDERS CHASE: SA, 200 kilometres/120 miles south of Adelaide on Kangaroo Island. Eucalyptus forests, ferns, kangaroos, duck-billed platypuses, geese, parrots and koalas. On an off-shore island, seals and seabirds. Open: all year round. Information centre, camping, accommodation, walking, fishing, swimming.

KAKADU NATIONAL PARK: NT, 250 kilometres/155 miles east of Darwin. Coastal plains, mangrove tidal flats, flood plains. Herons, pelicans, swans, vultures, sea eagles, aquatic plants, rock paintings. Open: May to October. Camping, accommodation, walking, fishing. *40, 41*

KATHERINE GORGE: NT, 30 kilometres/ 19 miles northeast of Katherine. Katherine River flows between deep canyon-like cliffs through a series of gorges. Aboriginal paintings, abundant animal life, crocodiles, birds, reptiles, kangaroos. Open: from May to October. Information centre, camping, accommodation, walking, fishing, swimming.

KOSCIUSKO NATIONAL PARK: NSW, 490 kilometres/305 miles southwest of Sydney. Mountain scenery around Australia's highest mountain. Winter ski area, wild flowers and eucalyptus forests. Open: all year round. Information centre, camping, accommodation, marked hiking tracks, fishing, swimming.

Grass trees, simply called "black boys" by the Australians.

LIZARD ISLAND NATIONAL PARK: The Great Barrier Reef. Coral islands with underwater scenery that can be viewed from glass-bottomed boats. Open: May to November. Information centre, swimming, snorkelling and scuba-diving.

NAMBUNG NATIONAL PARK: WA, 200 kilometres/120 miles north of Perth. The Pinnacles Desert with fascinating limestone pinnacles. Open: all year round. Walking, fishing, swimming.

SOUTHWEST NATIONAL PARK: TAS, 110 kilometres/68 miles west of Hobart. Unspoilt coastline with mountain scenery. Numerous glacial lakes, waterfalls, forests of birch, ash, beech, moorland

with heather, mosses, lichen and fungi. Open: November to February. Information centre, camping, walking, fishing, swimming.

STURT NATIONAL PARK: on the border of NSW, QLD and SA. Desert outback country with waterholes. Sparse desert vegetation, red and grey kangaroos. Open: November to March.

ULURU NATIONAL PARK: NT, 430 kilometres/267 miles southwest of Alice Springs. Open landscape of sandplains, dunes and mulga woodland with the monoliths of Ayers Rock and The Olgas. Aboriginal rock paintings. Open: May to October. Information centre, camping, accommodation, walking, swimming.

WILSON PROMONTORY: VIC, 250 kilometres/155 miles southeast of Melbourne. Southern tip of the continent, its granite slopes being all that is left of the former land bridge to Tasmania. Sharp-edged mountains rise above 650 metres/2,133 feet. Sandy beaches and dunes, fern gullies and koalas. Open: November to February. Information centre, camping, accommodation, walking, fishing, swimming.

Information concerning all of Australia's national parks can be obtained from the Australian Tourist Commissions or from the Australian National Parks and Wildlife Service, 217 Northbourne Avenue, Turner, ACT 2601.

LIST OF SOURCES AND ILLUSTRATIONS

Glenda Adams, "A Snake Down Under", in *The Hottest Night of the Century*. Sydney: Angus and Robertson Limited, 1979.

Bruce Chatwin, *Songlines*. London: Jonathan Cape, 1987.

William Dampier, *A Voyage to New Holland in the Year 1699*, in *Dampier's Voyages*, ed. J. Masefield. London: 1906.

Ernest Giles, *Australia Twice Traversed. . . .* London: 1889.

Mary Gilmore, "She was a Scented Land", in *Old Days, Old Ways*. Sydney: Angus and Robertson Limited, 1934.

Rachel Biddulph Henning, *The Letters of Rachel Henning*, ed. David Adams. Sydney: Angus and Robertson Limited, 1969.

Jan Morris, *Journeys*. Oxford: Oxford University Press, 1984. © Jan Morris 1984.

Charles Stuart, *Narrative of an Expedition into Central Australia*. London: 1849.

John McDouall Stuart, *The Journals of John McDo'uall Stuart during the Years 1858, 1859, 1860, 1861 and 1862,* ed. W. Hardman. London: 1864.

Abel Janzoon Tasman, *An Account of Several Late Voyages to the South and North, by Sir John Narborough, Captain Jasmen Tasman, Captain John Wood, and Frederick Marten of Hamburgh*. London: 1694.

Peter Egerton Warburton, *Journey across the Western Interior of Australia*. London: 1875.

We would like to thank all copyright holders and publishers for their kind permission to reprint. In a few cases, we were not able to find out who the copyright holders are, despite having made intensive efforts to do so. Those to whom this applies are asked to contact us.

DESTINATION AUSTRALIA
WINDSOR BOOKS INTERNATIONAL, 1992

©1991 by Verlag C.J. Bucher GmbH
Munich and Berlin
Translation: Nicholas H. Lloyd
Editor: Karen Lemiski
Anthology: Carmel Finnan, Karen Lemiski
All rights reserved
Printed and bound in Germany
ISBN 1 874111 07 3